WITHDRAWN

AMAZING SUPER SIMPLE INVENTIONS

SUPER SIMPLE

AUTOMOBILE
PROJECTS

INSPIRING & EDUCATIONAL
SCIENCE ACTIVITIES

ALEX KUSKOWSKI

Consulting Editor, Diane Craig, M.A./Reading Specialist

Super Sandcastle

An Imprint of Abdo Publishing
abdopublishing.com

abdopublishing.com

Published by Abdo Publishing, a division of ABDO, PO Box 398166, Minneapolis, Minnesota 55439. Copyright © 2016 by Abdo Consulting Group, Inc. International copyrights reserved in all countries. No part of this book may be reproduced in any form without written permission from the publisher. Super SandCastle™ is a trademark and logo of Abdo Publishing.

Printed in the United States of America, North Mankato, Minnesota
062015
092015

THIS BOOK CONTAINS
RECYCLED MATERIALS

Editor: Liz Salzmann
Content Developer: Nancy Tuminelly
Cover and Interior Design and Production: Mighty Media, Inc.
Photo Credits: Library of Congress, Mighty Media, Inc., Shutterstock, Wikicommons

The following manufacturers/names appearing in this book are trademarks: 3M™, Crayola®, Duracell®, Energizer®, X-ACTO®

Library of Congress Cataloging-in-Publication Data

Kuskowski, Alex, author
  Super simple automobile projects : inspiring & educational science activities / Alex Kuskowski ; consulting editor, Diane Craig, M.A./Reading specialist.
     pages cm -- (Amazing super simple inventions)
  Audience: K to grade 4.
  ISBN 978-1-62403-729-0
  1. Ford, Henry, 1863-1947--Juvenile literature. 2. Automobiles--Experiments-- Juvenile literature. 3. Automobiles--Models--Juvenile literature. 4. Automobiles- -History--Juvenile literature. 5. Inventions--Juvenile literature. I. Craig, Diane, editor. II. Title. III. Series: Kuskowski, Alex. Amazing super simple inventions.
  TL147.K87 2016
  629.222078--dc23
                    2014049930

Super SandCastle™ books are created by a team of professional educators, reading specialists, and content developers around five essential components—phonemic awareness, phonics, vocabulary, text comprehension, and fluency—to assist young readers as they develop reading skills and strategies and increase their general knowledge. All books are written, reviewed, and leveled for guided reading and early reading intervention programs for use in shared, guided, and independent reading and writing activities to support a balanced approach to literacy instruction.

To Adult Helpers

The projects in this title are fun and simple. There are just a few things to remember to keep kids safe. Some projects require the use of sharp or hot objects. Also, kids may be using messy materials such as glue or paint. Make sure they protect their clothes and work surfaces. Review the projects before starting, and be ready to assist when necessary.

....

KEY SYMBOLS

Watch for these warning symbols in this book. Here is what they mean.

HOT!
You will be working with something hot. Get help!

SHARP!
You will be working with a sharp object. Get help!

CONTENTS

AUTOMOBILES

AN INTRODUCTION

Look out your window at the street. One of the first things you will see is a car. Before 1900, that picture was very different.

When cars were first invented they were expensive. Only a few people could afford them. Henry Ford changed that. He made it so many people could have a car!

PARTS OF AN AUTOMOBILE

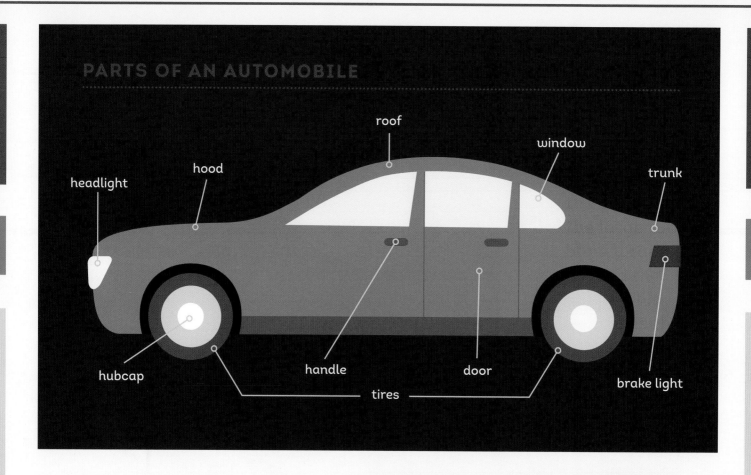

roof

window

headlight

hood

trunk

hubcap

handle

door

brake light

tires

Learn more about Ford and the car. Craft your own cars. Do experiments. Discover the car for yourself!

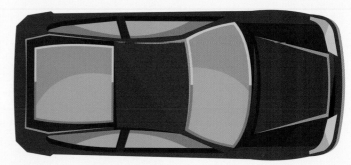

HENRY FORD

Henry Ford started the Ford Motor Company. His company started making cars in 1903.

Ford changed the way people made machines. His company was the first to use a moving **assembly line**.

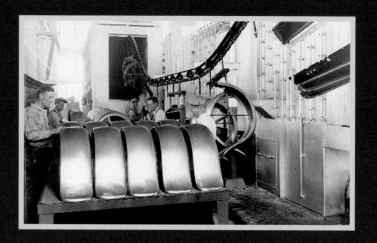

He used an **assembly line** to make cars. In the line, everyone had one job. They built each car piece by piece. Together they could make cars quickly. Ford could sell his cars for less money. This meant many more people could buy a car!

OTHER IMPORTANT PEOPLE

THOMAS PARKER

He invented the first electric car. It used rechargeable **batteries**.

NICOLAS CUGNOT

He invented the steam car. It went 2.5 miles per hour (4 kmh).

KARL BENZ

He invented the **gasoline**-powered car.

THEN TO NOW

A TIMELINE OF THE AUTOMOBILE

Karl Benz invented the motor car. It was the first car with a **gas** engine.

Ransom E. Olds started the Olds Motor Vehicle Company. They made the Oldsmobile.

Nicolas Cugnot invented the steam car. It was the first car.

| 1769 | 1884 | 1885 | 1896 | 1897 | 1903 |

Thomas Parker built a practical electric car.

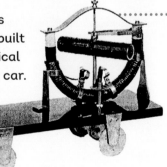

The Ford Quadricycle was the first vehicle developed by Henry Ford.

Henry Ford started the Ford Motor Company.

WHY THE FORD MODEL T?

It was fast, cheap, and sturdy. It could drive on dirt roads and fields. It looked like an expensive car. Ford sold more than 15 million Model Ts. Everyone wanted a Ford!

Seat belts were added to cars.

The Ford Motor Company started making the Model T.

The first highway was built in Italy.

1908   **1913**   **1924**   **1959**   **1997**

Ford started using a moving **assembly line**. Cars became something everyone could buy.

Cars started going green. Toyota built the Prius. It runs on **gas** and electricity.

BE AN INVENTOR

LEARN HOW TO THINK LIKE AN INVENTOR!

Inventors have a special way of working. It is a series of steps called the Scientific Method. Follow the steps to work like an inventor.

THE SCIENTIFIC METHOD

1. QUESTION

What question are you trying to answer? Write down the question.

2. GUESS

Try to guess the answer to your question. Write down your guess.

3. EXPERIMENT

Think of a way to find the answer. Write down the steps.

KEEP TRACK

There's another way to be just like an inventor. Inventors make notes about everything they do. So get a notebook. When you do an experiment, write down what happens in each step. It's super simple!

4. MATERIALS

What supplies will you need? Make a list.

5. ANALYSIS

Do the experiment. What happened? Write down the results.

6. CONCLUSION

Was your guess correct? Why or why not?

MATERIALS

AA battery

balloons

beads

black foam core

C battery

clear tape

copper wire

duct tape

hot glue gun & glue sticks

LED lights

neodymium magnets

painter's tape

Here are some of the **materials** that you will need.

paper clips

pliers

propeller

rubber bands

screw

small cardboard box

straws

watch battery

wooden craft sticks

wooden dowels

wooden nickels

X-Acto knife

BALLOON CAR

Blow away the competition!

MATERIALS: small cardboard box, acrylic paint, foam paintbrush, ruler, pencil, X-Acto knife, scissors, 2 wooden dowels, 2 straight straws, 3 bendable straws, 4 wooden nickels, hot glue gun & glue sticks, balloon, tape

Cars have been powered by many different kinds of energy. The first car was powered by steam. Today's cars are powered by **gasoline** and electricity.

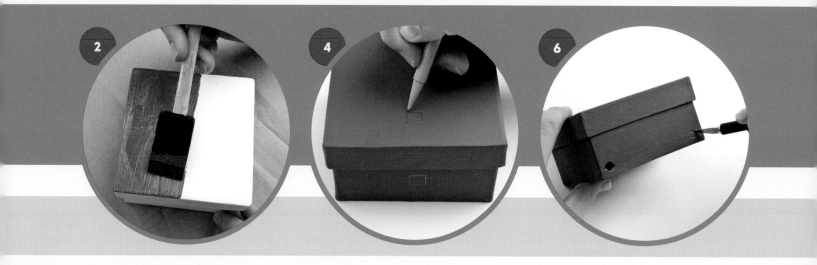

MAKE A BALLOON-POWERED CAR

① Paint the box white. Let it dry.

② Paint the box a bright color. Let it dry.

③ Draw a square about ½ inch (1.25 cm) wide in the center of a short side of the box.

④ Draw another square on the top of the box about 1 inch (2.5 cm) from the edge.

⑤ Draw a small circle near each bottom corner of the long sides of the box.

⑥ Cut out the squares and circles using an X-Acto knife.

continued on next page

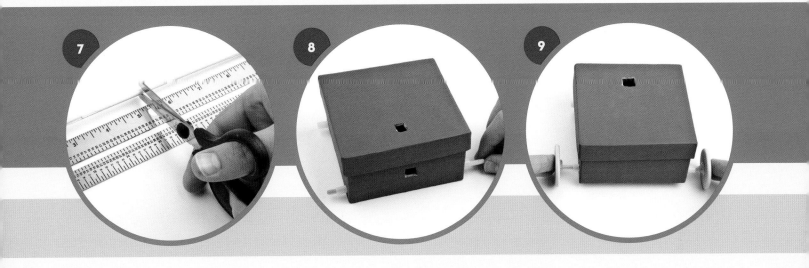

MAKE A BALLOON-POWERED CAR (CONTINUED)

7 Measure a short side of the box. Add ½ inch (1.25 cm) to the measurement. Cut the dowels and straight straws to the final length. Trim ¼ inch (.6 cm) off of each straw.

8 Push a straw through each set of corner holes. Push a dowel through each straw.

9 Hot glue a wooden nickel to each end of the dowels.

10 Group the bendable straws together. Pull the balloon over one end of the straws.

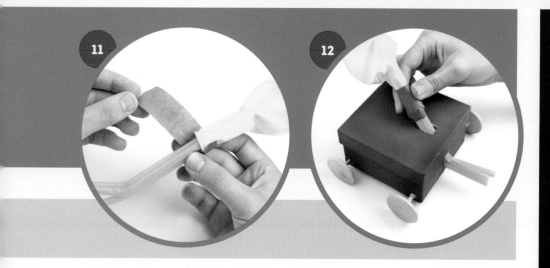

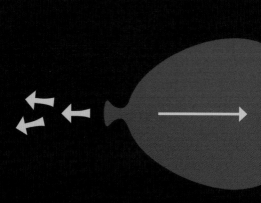

11 Tape the end of the balloon to the straws. Cover the end of the balloon so no air gets in.

12 Push the other end of the straws through the top hole on the box. Push the straws through to the side hole.

13 Blow into the straws until the balloon fills up. Hold your fingers over the straw ends. Set the car on the floor. Then let it go.

HOW DOES IT WORK?

The car you just made is powered by air! The air in the balloon moves out through the straws. The air goes out the back of the car. The movement of the air pushes the car forward.

WINDUP CAR

Get wound up in this car!

MATERIALS: black foam core, ruler, X-Acto knife, pencil, 2 straws, scissors, duct tape, 4 small rubber bands, 4 large rubber bands, 4 wooden nickels, hot glue gun & glue sticks, 2 wooden dowels, paper clip, weight (such as a box of crayons)

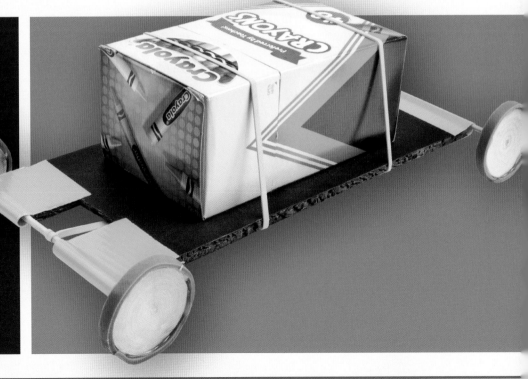

Different kinds of energy can move a car. One kind of energy is stored energy. Stored energy works like a **battery**. It holds power to use later.

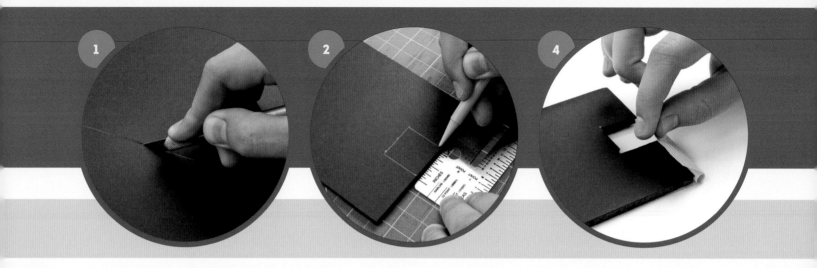

MAKE A WINDUP CAR

① Cut a rectangle out of foam core. Make it 4 inches (10 cm) by 9 inches (23 cm).

② Draw a 1-inch (2.5 cm) square in the center of a short side of the rectangle. Cut out the square.

③ Cut a straw into two 1½-inch (4 cm) pieces. Cut another straw 4 inches (10 cm) long.

④ Tape the short straws on each side of the square cutout. Tape the long straw to the other end of the rectangle.

⑤ Put two small rubber bands around the foam core. Put them about 2 inches (5 cm) apart.

continued on next page

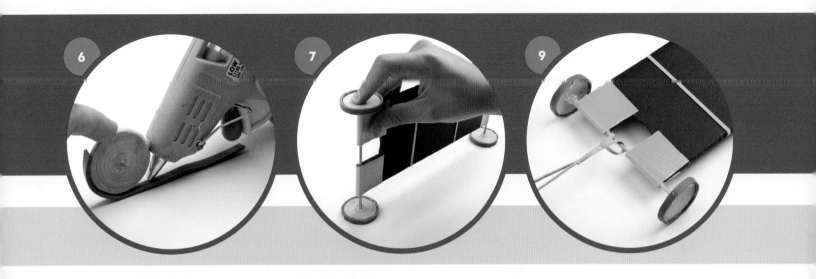

MAKE A WINDUP CAR (CONTINUED)

⑥ Cut a large rubber band to fit around the edge of a wooden nickel. Hot glue the band in place to make a wheel. Repeat for each wooden nickel.

⑦ Cut two 5-inch (13 cm) pieces of wooden dowel. Push a dowel through the long straw. Hot glue a wooden nickel to each end of the dowel. Let the glue dry. Repeat with the other dowel and the short straws.

⑧ Tie the two remaining small rubber bands together.

⑨ Tie one of the rubber bands around the dowel where the square is cut out.

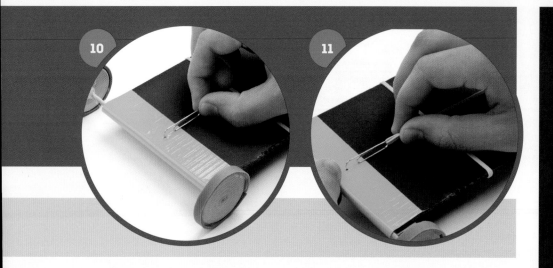

10 Straighten one section of the paper clip. Push it through the foam core near the long straw.

11 Attach the other end of the joined rubber bands to the paper clip.

12 Turn the car over so the paper clip is underneath. Set the weight on top of the car. Use the small rubber bands to hold it on.

13 Wind up the car by pulling it backwards. The end with the long straw is the front. Then let it go.

HOW DOES IT WORK?

When you pull the car back, the large rubber band wraps around the dowel. This stretches the rubber band. It creates and stores energy. When you let go, the rubber band unwinds. It takes the stored energy and uses it. The car rolls forward.

PROPELLER CAR

Wind it up and watch it go!

MATERIALS: 2 wooden craft sticks, hot glue gun & glue sticks, ruler, 2 paper clips, painter's tape, scissors, 4 large rubber bands, 4 wooden nickels, 2 wooden dowels, straw, pencil, thick card stock, propeller, medium bead, small rubber band

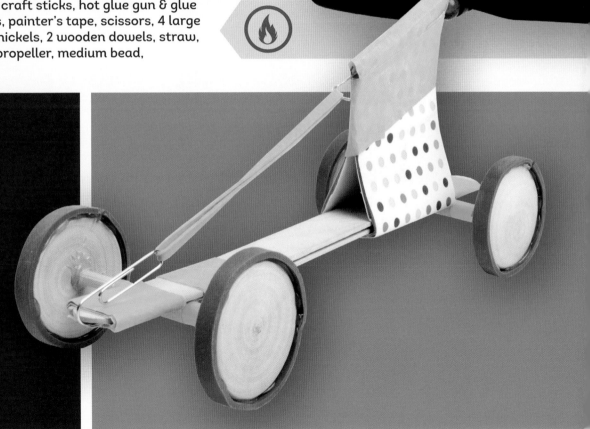

This car uses stored energy like the Windup Car *(see page 18)*. There are all kinds of ways to store energy. This car uses a **propeller**.

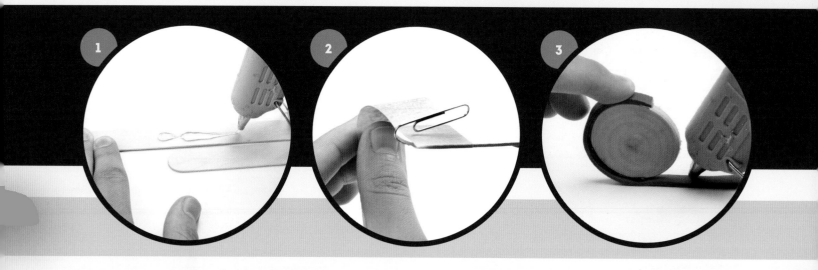

MAKE A PROPELLER CAR

....

1 Hot glue the craft sticks together. Leave 2 inches (5 cm) sticking out each end. This is the car's body.

2 Pull the end of a paper clip out slightly. Tape it to one end of the craft sticks. This is the front of the car.

3 Cut a large rubber band to fit around the edge of a wooden nickel. Hot glue the band in place to make a wheel. Repeat for each wooden nickel.

4 Cut two 2½-inch (6 cm) pieces of wooden dowel. Cut two 1½-inch (4 cm) pieces of straw. Cut another piece of straw 2 inches (5 cm) long. Put the dowel pieces through the small straw pieces.

continued on next page

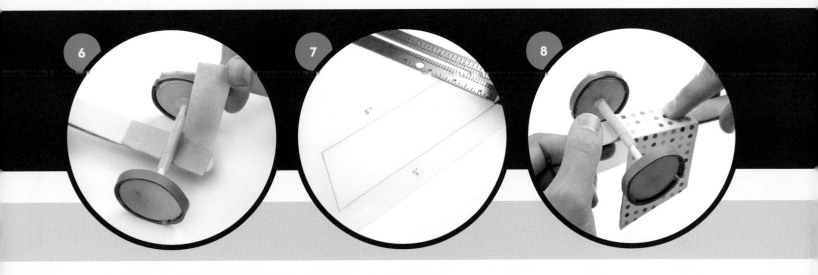

MAKE A PROPELLER CAR (CONTINUED)

⑤ Hot glue a wheel to each end of the wooden dowels. Let the glue dry.

⑥ Set one set of wheels across one end of the craft sticks. Tape the straw to the craft sticks. Tape the other wheels to the other end the same way.

⑦ Draw a **trapezoid** on card stock. Make it 2 inches (5 cm) high, 5 inches (12.5 cm) long on one side, and 7 inches (18 cm) long on the other side. Cut out the trapezoid.

⑧ Wrap the trapezoid around the craft sticks near the back wheels. Put the longest edge closest to the wheels. Hot glue it in place.

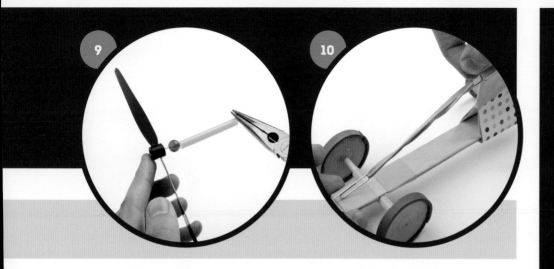

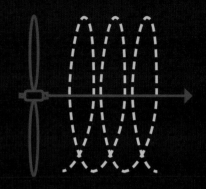

9 Straighten a paper clip with the pliers. Bend ¼ inch (.6 cm) of one end to the side. Push the other end of the paper clip through the **propeller**. Pull it until the bent end catches. Hot glue the paper clip in place. Let it dry. Put a bead and the last piece of straw on the paper clip. Bend the end to hold them in place.

10 Tape the straw to the top of the **trapezoid**. **Attach** the small rubber band to both paper clips. Turn the propeller to wind it up. Then let go and watch your car move!

Turning the propeller twists the rubber band. The twisted rubber band holds energy. When you let the car go, the rubber band untwists. The propeller spins. That moves the car forward.

MINI MOTORS

Get your motor running!

MATERIALS: copper wire, ruler, pliers, 4 neodymium magnets, AA battery, watch battery, 4 small LED lights, clear tape, 1½-inch (4 cm) screw, C battery

The motor in your car is like a giant **battery**. Batteries store a lot of energy. They help run your car.

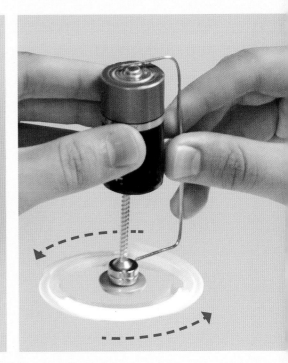

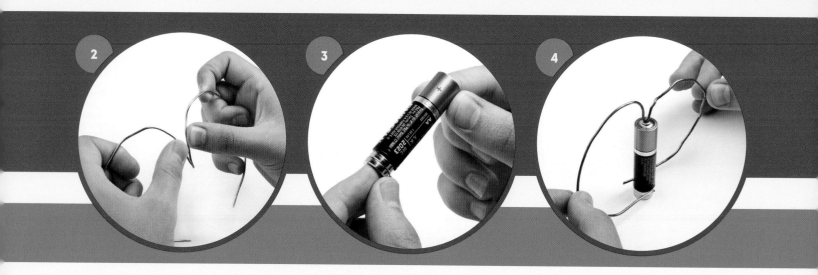

MAKE A SIMPLE SPINNING MOTOR

(1) Cut a piece of copper wire 16 inches (40 cm) long with the pliers. Use the pliers to bend the wire in half.

(2) Hold the middle of the copper wire with the ends facing up. Bend the ends down. Make a heart shape.

(3) Put two magnets on the **negative pole** of a AA **battery**. Set it on a table with the magnets on the bottom.

(4) Balance the middle of the copper wire on the **positive pole** of the battery. Move the ends until they touch the sides of the magnets. Let go and watch the wire spin!

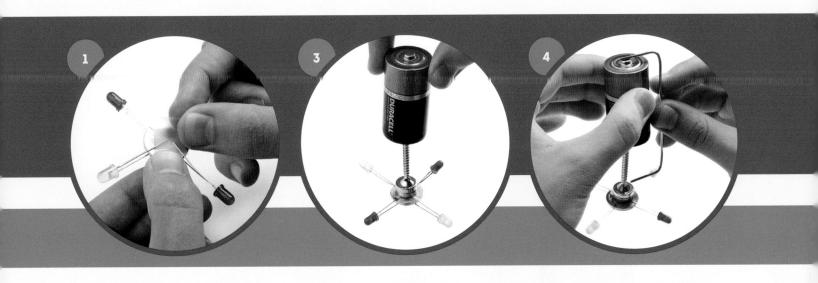

MAKE A MINI LED MOTOR

❶ Put the watch **battery** between the wires of each LED light. Put the short wires on the **negative pole** of the battery. Put the long wires on the **positive pole** of the battery. Tape the LED wires to the battery.

② Cut a piece of copper wire 5 inches (13 cm) long. Bend ¼ inch (.6 cm) of each end to the side.

❸ Set two magnets on top of the watch battery. Set the flat end of the screw on top of the magnets. Touch the flat end of the C battery to the top of the screw.

❹ Hold the motor above a flat surface. Touch one end of the wire to the top of the C battery. Touch the other end to the magnets. Watch the lights spin!

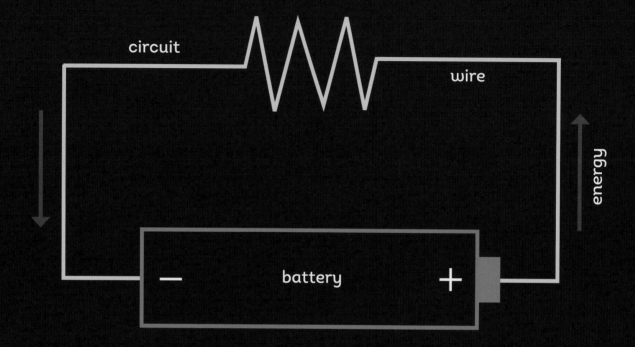

circuit

wire

energy

– battery +

HOW DOES IT WORK?

The motors you made are simple. The metal wire makes a circuit with the **batteries**. The circuit carries energy. It causes the wire in the Spinning Motor to move. It makes the lights in the Mini LED Motor move!

CONCLUSION

Automobiles are part of daily life. They are everywhere, but do you know how they really work? This book is the first step in discovering what's under the hood. There is a lot more to find out.

Learn about what runs on the road! Look online or at the library. Think of automobile crafts and experiments you can do on your own.

Put on your scientist thinking cap and go on a learning journey!

QUIZ

① What kind of line did Ford use to make cars quickly?

② The first car was powered by electricity. **TRUE OR FALSE?**

③ Name two reasons why the Ford Model T was so popular.

THINK ABOUT IT!

How do you think Ford's car changed the world?
How would life be different without the car?

Answers: 1. Assembly line   2. False   3. Pick two: It was fast, cheap, and sturdy.

GLOSSARY

assembly line – a way of making something in which the item moves from worker to worker until it is finished.

attach – to join or connect.

battery – a small container filled with chemicals that makes electrical power.

gasoline – a liquid that can burn that is used to power engines. *Gas* is short for *gasoline*.

material – something needed to make or build something else.

negative pole – the end of a battery that energy flows into when used in a circuit.

positive pole – the end of a battery that energy flows out of when used in a circuit.

propeller – a device with turning blades used to move a vehicle such as an airplane or a boat.

trapezoid – a shape with four sides. Two of the sides are parallel, but have different lengths. The other two sides are the same length, but not parallel.